Defiant!
Redefining Singleness at
30+

ETHLEEN SAWYERR

Copyright © 2020 by Ethleen Sawyerr

All rights reserved. This book, or any portion thereof, may not be reproduced or used in any manner without the express written permission of the author or publisher, except for the use of brief quotations in a book review.

Printed in the United States of America
First Printing, 2020
ISBN 978-1-7345023-0-5

www.ethleenwrites.com

To Charlotte, Chelsea, Grace, Kimber, Serena, and countless young women born to defy the mold. The greatness within you will change this world.

To Andrew, the man who consistently demonstrates what it means to be a gracious husband, loving father, and prayerful child of God.

ACKNOWLEDGEMENTS

This book would not have been made possible without these fabulous individuals.

Anna – Thanks for holding me accountable to finish this book. Those early morning "pep texts" and mid-day check-ins were annoying, but they were absolutely necessary! Your friendship is invaluable.

Claudette and Aunt Marcia - Thank you for your constructive feedback and encouragement along the way.

Robin Devonish – Your advice and input took this book to a new level. Thank you for taking the time, treating my story with care, and cheering me on in the process. Every aspiring author should check out www.robinedevonish.com.

Heavenly Father – You know that I've enjoyed these last seven (or so) years of anonymity. This book was written as an act of obedience to You, the Lover of my soul. Thank You, Father, for never leaving my side and always being the one constant in my life.

CONTENTS

Preface 1
Chapter 1: Redefining Singleness at 30+ 3
Chapter 2: Who Sinned? 7
Chapter 3: When the One You Want Disappoints............ 15
Chapter 4: Goodbye, Marriage? 25
Chapter 5: Friday Night Fears.. 33
Chapter 6: Being the Unwelcomed Stranger...................... 39
Chapter 7: Friendless 47
Chapter 8: Putting on the Weight Again 57
Chapter 9: Crooked Crown 61
Chapter 10: Stand Tall, Anomaly 67
Chapter 11: No More Chasing.. 71
Words from the Author 77

PREFACE

Growing up, I knew I wasn't like my peers. While they were dating, smoking, and engaging in "typical" teenage activities, I was doing ministry in nursing homes, delivering gifts to children whose parents were incarcerated, and leading Bible studies. I can't quite put it into words, but I just knew that my life was meant for a specific purpose bigger than myself. In my early teens, a well-known preacher/evangelist told me that I was destined for greatness. I thought it was just some cliché he told all young people, but maybe he knew something I didn't.

I carried the dream to open schools and orphanages in the developing world with me for a long time. Almost every decision I've made in life has been with this goal, which came from a deep desire in me to provide children around the world with access to formal education, in mind. I know the power of learning and wanted them to be able to see how life-changing it can be. This seemed like a lofty goal, but I set out on the journey to make my dreams come true.

The road has had its own hurdles and called for sacrifices along the way. Somewhere on my journey, I found myself at the age of 29, running a business, leading some other organizations, and still going hard for my dreams.

Suddenly, I had a series of reflective moments when I took stock of all that had "passed me by." *Defiant! Redefining Singleness at 30+* was birthed out of a strong need to share with women, particularly the young women I have had the privilege to help raise in varying degrees, the joys and pains of certain pivotal life moments. I wrote this book with those young ladies, as well as my unborn daughter, in mind. It is my way of speaking truths into their lives in the event they find themselves at a certain age and with a desire for marriage, but there are no potential suitors knocking on their doors.

This book is for the woman who is beyond 30 and still holding out hope that God has not forgotten about her secret longing to become a wife and mother. These chapters were written for the woman who is approaching 30 and feels like an entire season of life has passed her by because she's nearing that dreaded age and still goes to an empty home each night. It is for the young lady who is resolved to go it alone but finds herself in that place where she is tempted to settle for just "any random dude" or find comfort in a different kind of Love.

No matter what stage of this journey you are on, I pray this book will challenge you to go on new adventures, get to know yourself at a deeper level, and draw closer to God.

Let's redefine singleness together.

REDEFINING SINGLENESS AT 30+

It's here. The day you never imagined would come. Everyone's "day" won't look the same, but it will probably evoke similar feelings of loneliness, disappointment, and despair. What do I mean? There will come a time (it may have already taken place) where it dawns on you that you, my dear, are 30+ and single. The age of 30 seems more arbitrary to me than anything else. I think it's more about reaching that point in your life when you realize that you're doing amazing things but have no one to share them with when you go home at the end of the day. Yes, you have friends, family, and followers who are cheering you on. But your heart's desire is for an intimate companion to take part in the joys and sorrows of the journey with you.

Now that I'm at this point, being 30 and single doesn't quite seem like the scary monster I once thought it was. I literally feared reaching this day because I thought everything about my life would change. Once I turned 30, I imagined my skin would start to become wrinkly, my ability to "hang" with younger friends would become almost nonexistent, and a new level of "maturity" would automatically kick in. I was wired to believe that this was the age of all ages, when I would be at the peak of my game and have everything I desired in life. Do you understand what I'm saying? I guess somewhere along the way, I convinced myself that by the age of 30 I was supposed to have and be able to eat my proverbial cake. More specifically, I believed I would be in a committed marriage or long-term relationship with the intent of walking down the aisle as quickly as possible. That's not my reality.

My "day" snuck up on me unexpectedly as I reminisced about my graduate school experience. In undergrad, I always thought I would get married while in pursuit of a graduate degree. Actually, I thought I would get the PhD right away and be done with higher education completely. I'd be struggling to complete my dissertation, then he (my fiancé or husband) would be the one motivating me to make it to the finish line. The day I walked across the stage to receive my diploma, he would be the one standing up and sharing in that victorious moment with me. Isn't that cute? Again, that's not my reality.

On my "day," my mind was consumed with the laundry list of things I had done by myself. I wallowed in the fact that he has missed out on so much of my life and vice versa. Why would God do that to me when He knows how much I long to be a wife and mother?

In one brief moment, it was like every other aspect of my life became inconsequential because this particular area remained unfulfilled. Well, those musings came and went. If I'm honest, there are still occasions when the feelings from that "day" sneak in, but I do my best to remind myself that the notion of automatically becoming a spinster at age 30 doesn't exist. Life doesn't end at that number. My life isn't insignificant because I'm still single. My life on earth ceases to exist when God calls me home. Until then, I make the most of all He's blessed me with.

You may be older than 30 and waiting for God to make good on His promise. Dear friend, I encourage you to keep trekking because He can do anything but fail. You may be nearing 30 and ready to give up completely because the possibility of marriage doesn't look like it's in your immediate future and the options for potential spouses are **beyond** slim. I implore you to shift your focus because you have so much going for you currently that requires your attention. Then, you might be like me and 30 is at your door. I ask you to join me in reminding yourself that we are all in this together. You have sisters around the world living in that same space who are rooting for you to make it and fulfill your higher calling.

Settling for whomever comes along seems so simple, but it can lead to a life filled with unnecessary regret. I sometimes wish I could accept the proposal made by the next man who walks into my life or even displays a semblance of interest. However, I have an idea of where God is leading me and the caliber of a man I need (not the one I want) to continue the work He's begun in me.

I often remind myself that my marriage is not just about fulfilling my (oftentimes desperate) longing for a companion; it is also about the legacy I will leave for my children and generations that follow. I **have** to be selective; this is the man I will partner with to raise sons, daughters, and grandchildren who will leave a mark on the world. That's kind of a big deal, don't you think? I do. That's why I can't choose just any man.

Since we're all at different stages and experiencing similar thoughts or situations, why don't we band together? Let's redefine singleness at 30+ and all the ridiculous expectations placed on us as (still) single women to boldly live the one life we've been given to the glory of God.

Friend, you were never meant to be the mold. You were created to break it.

WHO SINNED?

"Why are you still single?"
"What's wrong with you?"
"Why hasn't any man snatched you up yet?"

As a single woman approaching or well beyond the age of 30, being asked a barrage of questions like these (and more) is the norm. In our culture, being a woman who is single and eligible is treated like a crime. To me, it's like people equate my lack of having a spouse at this age with sin. It's as if I have a major character flaw because a man has not stopped to notice how awesome I am and made me his wife. Do you feel that way at times?

I've found that one thing people who bombard me with this line of questioning don't get is that I am more than content in my singleness. They assume that I'm unhappy because I don't have someone. What if I didn't want to get married? What if I enjoy being single and unattached? It never seems to dawn on them that some people prefer the single life. I mean, with the current divorce rate as it stands, marriage appears to be a rushed process that many enter in only to discover they chose the wrong partner.

One other possibility that's often overlooked is that me being single until this point is part of God's will. There's a passage in John chapter 9 where Jesus and his disciples encounter a man born blind. The disciples ask Jesus if the man was blind because of his own sins or because of the sins of his parents. Jesus tells them that neither party sinned. The man's blindness was intentional to serve a purpose for that very day in history when the power of God's son would be displayed for the masses to see.

Did you catch that? This man lived his entire life with the inability to see because God had destined that his sight would be given to him by Jesus Christ. Meaning, there was an appointed time for him to receive his sight, but that time was on God's schedule, not his. Even greater than that, his blindness served a purpose because everyone knew about it. When Jesus stepped into the scene and gave the man his vision, the formerly blind man had a testimony that no one could tell him was false. He tells the Pharisees that God doesn't listen to sinners. Rather, He pays attention to those who do His will. Since it was not every day that someone opened the eyes of a blind man, only someone sent by God could do it (John 9:31-33). It's incredible! This miracle changed at least three lives that day (the man, his mother, and his father); his pre-ordained blindness served a purpose to glorify the Son of God.

What if we shifted the way we viewed our singleness? Maybe if we did, then the world would stop treating singleness like it's a curse. After all, Paul says that he desires for us to remain single so that we can focus more on God (1 Corinthians 7). What if our singleness is God's way of allowing us to fulfill a purpose and accomplish those dreams that don't require a spouse?

Can I tell you something? Growing up, I had some audacious goals. I mean, the type of dreams I thought only God could make come true because my circumstances constantly highlighted what I lacked. I desired to have multiple degrees, live in different places, and be my own boss. I can't even tell you today what it was that brought those specific goals to my mind in the first place, but I secretly held them close. While I was conjuring up these bold dreams, I wasn't sure if I'd even be able to obtain an undergraduate degree because of finances. I hated change, so the idea of moving around and being far from my father scared me to the core. I didn't even know what I would do that could bring in enough money to put food on the table and shelter over my head.

Do you know what? They have all come to fruition. I have been afforded opportunities that many of my peers have not. I currently hold two degrees, have lived in several places in the US, and own a growing business teaching all things related to the English language (a job that I love).

If truth be told, looking back, I see how one thing led to another. Having been born in Sierra Leone, my family immigrated to the US when I was young. Growing up in New Jersey, I was surrounded by people from a plethora of countries and cultures, which led to my love for languages. After my senior year of high school, I attended Howard University in Washington, DC to study English, education, and French. After Howard, I lived in Maryland, moved to Pennsylvania, then finally returned to Jersey for work. Later, my passion for languages and people took me across the country to Seattle, Washington to work with immigrant families. A few years later, I find myself living in Georgia and working with immigrants, individuals from disadvantaged communities, and entrepreneurs needing varying English services.

I can honestly say that I wouldn't have been able to do any of these things if I hadn't been single. You see, I determined in my heart some years ago that I wanted to start a family shortly after getting married. My children didn't necessarily need to come from my womb, but I wanted a home filled with them. Immediately after that first child entered the picture, I would be ready, willing, and able to forsake almost everything else to devote my life to raising him or her. This may not be the same for you, but I valued motherhood enough that I planned on doing this.

In fact, as I write, I am recalling a series of conversations with God where I asked Him to allow me to accomplish those same goals I mentioned earlier before settling down with a husband and children. (You know, we really should be careful what we pray for.) If I had known that praying those prayers would leave me single at age 30, with all I have going for me now, I would have prayed those prayers all the more.

God listens. He does care. I believe that He has blessed me with singleness to allow me to achieve certain dreams. Yes, I could have finished school, traveled the country, and started a business with a spouse and children by my side.

But I had specifically prayed for the ability to do all those things and be fully secure in who I am as an individual before I had to share my life with other people. Once a husband and children entered the picture, I didn't want to feel like I didn't do anything with my life.

Too often I meet women who tell me they got married young and regretted it. Some go as far as to implore me to take my time when it comes to dating and selecting a future spouse because they wish someone had cautioned them. They hear stories about my adventures and encourage me to make the most of my single years because marriage and children change everything. This is not to say that everyone should follow my path and totally forsake getting married when younger. I'm simply offering perspective that marriage is more about you and your readiness, not a specific age.

Perhaps we need to be having more conversations about the realities of marriage and the amount of work, prayer, and patience needed to make the union of two different people successful? It's a thought. Nonetheless, when a married friend or associate expresses his or her envy of my freedom in singleness, it stops me in my tracks to take stock of all I can do now that I may not be able to after "I do."

A few years ago, I was so fed up with being single at an age when most of my peers were either married or engaged that I created a list. (Yes, I like lists.) It started as a way for me to stick it to my future husband and show him all I was forced (unwillingly at times) to learn because he took his precious time finding me. The list ended up being a great reminder of all God has allowed me to accomplish in my life.

Some of the items on the list aren't particularly stellar to the rest of the world, but those who knew me growing up (and even now) would be shocked to find out all that I can do. Why? Because I was quite the prima donna who turned her nose down at just about any type of manual or blue-collar labor. It's amazing how we grow in seasons and only realize it after the fact.

I think it's wonderful (if I'm honest) that God blessed me with these years of singleness because I have proven to Him, myself, and my family that I can make it. Yes, it's been tough. Yes, there have been numerous sleepless nights filled with what seemed like endless tears. Yes, I've cried out to God for a helper during the journey. Nevertheless, if I got married tomorrow and something happened to my husband, our family would be ok. I know how to hold down multiple jobs at a time, can live on a budget, and am able to balance a checkbook. I can even do minor repairs around the house to save us a few dollars.

I applaud my father for raising an independent daughter. Both my parents played a role in who I am today, but I know that my father was intentional about how he raised me because his life circumstances taught him that I would need to know how to function on my own if I lost it all. He may not think I was paying attention when we had those conversations, but I remember them well. I used to hate my independence because I felt like men didn't approach me because they were turned off by it. Now, I know that it is something many women envy and desire.

Don't worry if you, too, are an independent woman because there is a man who will recognize it as one of your greatest assets. You see, singleness is not something bestowed on you because you sinned, and it's not an indicator that you are lacking in any way. Think back. Did you ever pray some audacious prayers like I did? Or maybe you asked God to use you to do some things that, when you stop and really think about it, would have been challenging to execute with a husband and family to care after? Perhaps God promised that He would use you to do some things for His glory that would change a generation, but marriage would cause you to divide your time and energy from getting them done His way?

Marriage isn't bad. What if He is saying "not now" because there is still some work for you to do in your single years? You're not still single because you sinned. I can only answer for myself, so please state your case before God. I'm still single because I purposely wanted to feel like I was "fulfilled" and secure in who I am and what God has given me to contribute to this world before the title of "mom" and "wife" replaced my identity for the better part of my life.

Can you take time to do some introspective work and identify why you are still single? Go ahead. Put a bookmark on this page and allow yourself a few minutes to meditate on this.

Defiant!

Here's the semi-complete list of things I have learned to do before my husband graces me with his presence. (I've intentionally omitted some key items because they're private and only for his eyes—on the off chance he gets his hands on this book.) How many of these things can you do (or have you done)? What would you add?

- Reconcile a bank account
- Repair someone's credit
- Buy a home
- Change a flat tire (after the roadside assistance warranty expires, of course)
- Change a faulty light switch
- Paint a room (several, in fact)
- Replace a light fixture
- Hand wash a car correctly

_____

_____

_____

_____

_____

_____

_____

_____

WHEN THE ONE YOU WANT DISAPPOINTS

Have you ever met someone whose existence was confirmation that God had not forgotten you? A person who stands out in the crowd simply by being himself and not caring what others think? The thought of him brings a smile to your face because if you had to create your ideal "type," he would be it. In fact, you're so infatuated with him that he becomes the one you want.

His name is Joseph. Every other man paled in comparison to him. I thought he was too good to be true. To be completely truthful, there were times when my excitement about him resulted in what some may consider borderline idolatry. Of course, I only realized this in hindsight, but I digress.

You see, when I got to a certain age, I began identifying the traits I desired in a spouse. Have you begun doing this? Maybe you want someone who speaks multiple languages. You might be adamant about becoming one with a man who is gifted musically. As my mind began to wander about the ideal attributes of my potential significant other, I started creating "the list." I think just about everyone has a list. Whether we call it that or not, we all have some idea of what we want in the person we decide to spend our lives with.

I created my list during my freshman year at Howard University. To be perfectly honest, I had created pseudo lists before that time. However, they never stuck; guys weren't on my priority list before college. They were nice to look at, but I was more focused on other things. My list was quite ambitious. I basically sought a man like my father, with a few additional things to suit my specific needs and lifestyle. Along the way, the list was modified to match my particular "season" in life. I became less vain and began to focus on the things most important to me: character, servanthood, faith, and more. This has probably happened to you, too.

As I've matured, I've realized that what I thought mattered in high school and college doesn't now. I wanted to be with someone who was kind, respectful, and commanding at the same time. Whenever he walked into a room, all eyes would shift to him when he began to speak. He'd be comfortable in the spotlight, but he would know when to step back and allow someone else to shine. My original list mandated that my potential spouse had to speak at least five languages, make a six-figure salary, be at least six feet tall, and have a heart for children.

Today, the only requirement from that list that still holds true is the last one. Why? Because the other stuff is inconsequential. If this fictional man only spoke two languages, I would still love him. If he only made a five-figure salary, our combined income would still be enough to provide for our family. If he didn't have to bend down and strain himself to kiss me, I'm sure we'd still be able to display our affection for each other. The one thing I know I wouldn't be able to deal with is being with someone who didn't love children. That makes sense because I want to build schools, open orphanages, and have a house full of young people. If a potential suitor told me he didn't like or want children, he would lose his status as "Mr. Possibly the One" and be sent packing.

After giving up on the idea of ever meeting a man who came anywhere close to my heart's desire, I stumbled upon Joseph. From afar, he was literally everything I had ever asked God for (minus the languages). He had the musical giftings, sense of humor, and a faith in God that bore fruit (John 15). The thing I loved most about him was that he taught God's Word; he is an incredibly gifted communicator. Beyond his good looks, his way with words made me melt. (I'm sure plenty of other women felt the same.)

For three years I secretly carried a torch for this man. It began with admiring him from afar to see if he was the real deal. Pretty soon, I learned we had mutual friends and occasionally ran into him at events. On more than one occasion, I was tempted to contact one friend to ask her about setting us up. In fact, I almost went through with it. However, God had made it abundantly clear that the only way I would know Joseph was the one was if he found me without me manipulating the situation.

I was so confident that God was orchestrating our paths into alignment; Joseph was the one. I held on to this belief, and it kept my mind occupied. It was pointless even wasting my time thinking about other men because I had already encountered the man who I could see myself spending forever with. There were even moments along the way when Joseph would post something on social media that gave me reassurance that our paths would eventually collide. To be honest, there were signs and acts of confirmation that made me believe wholeheartedly that Joseph was God's will for me.

In the past, when I met a man who piqued my interest, I'd go through the same process. First, I'd get all gung-ho and learn as much I could about him to make sure he checked off the necessary "boxes." Then, I'd talk him up to friends and associates to get their thoughts on our "matchability." After that, I'd position myself to be in places where he was so he could see me and have opportunities to engage in conversation.

Once that was done, a heavy dose of reality would kick in—I'd convince myself that there was something wrong with the man I was crushing on. I'd dig and dig until I found his fatal flaw. By "fatal flaw," I'm referring to the most miniscule personality quirk that I used as the reason to refrain from allowing the possibility of a romantic relationship to occur. It could be that he snored or wore outside shoes inside the house. Maybe he was socially awkward in specific circles because he'd never been in those contexts before and didn't know how to comport himself. It could even be that he had a deep country accent that forced me to listen intently when he spoke because, otherwise, I wouldn't be able to follow the conversation.

Joseph was none of those things; he was seemingly perfect (for me). That is, until I learned some troubling news that gave me cause to pause. Dear friend, be careful not to create a fantasy life for yourself that is free of pain and discomfort. We don't like to think about bad things happening to those we care for, but we live in a fallen world. Anything can happen to any of us at any time.

I was so distraught to hear about some of Joseph's battles with mental health. Then, there were the suggestive comments about his dealings with women. The talk wasn't necessarily scandalous, but it definitely made me apprehensive about continuing to long for a future with him. The man I once would have waited decades for was now just another joker in my mind. The last time I prayed for him, I cried so hard because it felt like I was carrying the weight of his mental health pain. It was such an eye-opening experience. I can't quite put it into words, but it felt like Joseph was choosing life again at the very moment that I was praying. Yet, the burden of knowing he was on the verge of making a different decision broke me. It was at that point that I saw him for who he was.

Without ever speaking a word to him about his love life, it was like I suddenly gained some insight into why he was still single. It wasn't because he was hard to love or had commitment issues. He needs a partner who is strong enough to wake up each day to cheer him on as he goes out into a world that is trying every which way to beat him down. Some days the world might win, and he'll come home feeling defeated and ready to make bad choices. His spouse must be the one to remind him of who God says he is, pray him through, and help guide him to the foot of the cross. That kind of woman isn't created overnight. She is the product of trials and tests that can sometimes take the better part of a lifetime.

In that moment in my room while I was praying for Joseph, I became aware of the weight of being with a man like him. If I had to get on my knees and pray to God like I did that day on a regular basis, I think I would go crazy. There was no way any man was worth all of that. I mean, if he truly was who God had for me, the Lord would have to rethink that selection. I made the decision that life with this man was not for me; Joseph was not my portion. Even though he was who I wanted, I gave up praying for God to make something happen between us.

Maybe it was a reckless choice. All I knew was that, if a union was His will, God would have to literally move mountains to bring us together. In the meantime, I stopped going to events I knew he would attend, unfollowed him on social media, and prayed fervently that God would "remove the taste of Joseph from my mouth."

To say that this was one of the hardest decisions ever would be an understatement. This man's existence literally revitalized my hope that God had not forgotten His promise to me of becoming a wife. I was pushing 30, many of my friends were married or in committed relationships, and I desperately needed to know that there was still hope for me. Joseph's life meant that what I desired in a man was attainable; I wasn't asking for the impossible. It also meant that I didn't have to settle.

Too many women enter adulthood thinking they have to make a bunch of concessions to get (and keep) a man. If for nothing else, knowing a man like Joseph exists reassures me that I should stand firm on what I desire in a spouse. He must have strong faith in Christ. He should be an excellent communicator. He must have the heart of a servant who doesn't seek outward praise. The list literally goes on.

More importantly, it may seem like you're asking for the world when you create your list. Just remember that your Father is the Creator of the universe, and He will not withhold any good thing from you when you walk in His ways (Psalm 84:11). Not too long ago, a friend reminded me of the passage in the Bible that talks about the things our earthly father gives to us and how God is able to give even better gifts. I know that if I asked for the moon and stars, God would give them to me.

Joseph is not an anomaly. There are more men like him out there who possess the traits on my list. There are men who fit the criteria you have established. Don't give up simply because you feel like you're getting older and the "pickings are slim." Do not compromise. When the one you want disappoints, there will be another because God will not make you a promise that He does not intend to fulfill.

There could be a number of reasons why God hasn't brought that other man into my life to replace Joseph. God could be working on my heart to build my faith and strengthen me to be a better prayer warrior for my future spouse. Maybe I gave up too quickly on Joseph, so God allowed us to separate to eventually bring us back together in a way only He knows how to do. Perhaps the Lord is working on Joseph through some of the mental health issues he deals with on a regular basis. Maybe there's a completely different man for me who just hasn't been brought into the mix. Regardless of the reason, I hold firm to the belief that God's way of orchestrating my love life is best.

Friend, do not be afraid to admit that you got it wrong about the one you believed was for you. Pray and seek God's wisdom about the matters of your heart. Your friends can only advise you to a certain point. If you want to know what your future holds, then you must turn to the One who holds your future in His hands. If God brings someone to you, praise Him. If He doesn't, praise Him all the same.

Society will tell you that you need a spouse to be happy and live a fulfilled life, but that is far from the truth. All you need is to be in the will of God. Paul was right when he said that it's better to remain single because we can give God our undivided attention (1 Corinthians 7). Communing with God is an incredible experience. I can't even find the words sometimes to express how I feel after spending time with Him.

Can I tell you something? Every so often, the thought crosses my mind that God enjoys my singleness because He treasures having me all to Himself. Does that sound silly? I think He feels the same about my spouse. It's almost like He's making the most of the limited moments He still has with us separately because there will come a day when He must let us go so that we can meet each other. We mean so much to Him. It's like He's taking in the precious one-on-one time before He has to share us. This suggestion isn't biblical, but that's how I think about it at times.

Don't worry about a spouse so much that you forget God. Remember what it was like when you first fell in love with our Savior. Think back to those daily prayers, chats, and Bible readings. He longs for your company more than you know.

GOODBYE, MARRIAGE?

I know who my husband is…sort of. Before you dismiss me as crazy, allow me to explain. Since undergrad, God has been revealing things to me about my spouse. He's a great orator, teaches the Word of God to others, and has a heart for service. Many of those characteristics were pretty obvious because they complement my personality well. But then I'd have these vivid dreams where God revealed very specific things about the man He has for me. Now, I don't necessarily ascribe to the belief that there is only one person in this entire world for you; instead, I believe that there are multiple potential spouses available to us. God gives us the choice of who to pick based on the path we decide to walk down.

There had been men in college who were ready to marry me, but I couldn't see myself being happy with them. In those days, I **chose** to be single. Did you catch that? When I was in the prime of my life (by the world's standards), I opted **not** to pursue any serious romantic relationships. Is that the case for you? What currently holds your attention as being the most important thing in life?

God has given me such specific insights about my future spouse that I dare not list them all for fear of random men popping up out of the woodworks posing as someone they are not. Friend, all I will say is that when this man makes his presence known, I'll know. Maybe that's why I found such comfort in Joseph. (Remember him?) There were numerous times when I just knew he had come from God. Just so we're clear, if God were to work His miracle in our lives, Joseph would still have a chance. But it would only take an act of God for that to happen.

It seems like once you begin to near 30, there's some unwritten rule that people are allowed to start pressuring you into marriage. Do not give them a foothold. Your life is not meant to follow their template. In fact, something these people don't tell you is that your marriage union isn't for you; it's for God. I would rather remain single and happy because I can constantly bask in the love of my Father than married, miserable, and unfulfilled.

If I had married any of those men from years ago, I'm confident that I'd either be divorced right now or cooped up in a mansion somewhere away from my family and living as a trophy wife. What kind of life would that be? How would God feel about me abandoning His will to please my flesh or society? When I counted the cost, I just couldn't handle the guilt of walking away from what I knew God was calling me to; His will for my life is so much better than my own. How do I know? He has been the one keeping me from the time I was born.

I can only write this book because of His grace. There's nothing spectacular about me or my life. The only thing I know for certain is that you will have moments when you feel like an outcast because those around you are getting married. You may even feel like something is wrong with you now because there are no suitors at your door. Say goodbye to the idea of marriage as you have seen it on TV and the false template about how your life should unfold.

If God wanted you married by now, you would be. Let go of those thoughts that you somehow messed up and let some decent potential husbands get away. There's no such thing as a "decent husband." If your heart's desire is for a man who fears God and treats you like the gift that you are, don't settle for someone who doesn't because you're concerned about your biological clock (or anything else for that matter).

Our spouse is supposed to love us like Christ loves the Church. If this man is unwilling to humble himself, seek godly wisdom, and fall on his knees to God about your relationship, he isn't the one. Move on and count yourself blessed that you were spared much heartache and wasted time. It's harsh and difficult to hear (or read) these words, but I wish we said them more often. What would happen if we watched and waited to see the fruit of a man who loved us like Christ loves the Church before walking down the aisle? I wonder how much lower the divorce rate would be if we took God at His word that He wouldn't withhold anything good from us.

At the end of the day, you want a man who loves and fears God because he knows the value of his commitment to you. There will be times when we behave irrationally and are unable to explain our actions. Some other men would flee when you have your "crazy girl moments," but the one God has will intercede on your behalf and turn to the Lord first to learn how best to love you through your mess.

What consumed your mind before the thought of marriage? What did you do prior to overthinking about who in your past you could try to rekindle a flame with? There's a lot more we can be doing with our time than trying to make something happen that God hasn't given us permission to pursue.

There's so much wisdom in the Scriptures. Remember that verse in Song of Solomon 8 about awakening love before its time? Why do you think we're told not to do that? Is it because the author knows how good love (and all that comes with it) is and wants to keep it from us? I don't think so. I think it's because the love that we've been created to give and receive is the most powerful of all. It is what causes us to lay down our lives for friends, undergo surgery to give up an organ for another, and abandon our dreams to make someone else's come true. If these are merely examples of what happens in a platonic love relationship, imagine what we would do for a romantic partner.

Friend, please take heed of my words. Don't rush into falling in love or convincing yourself that you are in love. Allow yourself time to move past the "feels" of your flesh and let a man's love manifest in his words and actions. Love is patient when you catch an attitude. Love respects you and your body, even when you don't. Love makes time to see you, despite having a busy schedule. If there is a man you desire to spend forever with, but it's always one excuse or another with him, run. Take it from me, if you are number three or four on his priority list, you will probably always be. (Although God can get a hold of a man and change his heart, trust that wonderful intuition you've been given when you suspect foul play.) The one who knows your worth will go out of his way to make you a priority, even if he has to drive 300 miles during the night just to see you off at the airport on your way to your six-month study abroad trip.

I know you want to be married. I do, too. But when I stop to think about the amount of energy and work required to make a marriage successful, I need to know that my future spouse is just as committed to the relationship.

The whole notion of a single woman 30 or beyond being a "lost cause" for romance seems like such a sham. God tells us to be fruitful and multiply (Genesis 1:28), but He never said that we had to do it by a certain age. If you're nearing that arbitrary number and aren't married, continue to live on. Your life won't end because you're 30 and single. Even as I write, I am living out that time in my own life. Nevertheless, I keep living. I've begun relearning sign language. My business is growing. I'm becoming a regular at a local gym. And I travel to visit friends across the country.

Please don't feel like you have to stop doing what you're doing because 30 is around the corner and the other side of the bed is empty. One day it will be filled, and you'll have some amazing stories to share about all you did before he came into the picture. If he's really cool, he'll probably be impressed by your tales and how you lived.

The desire to be someone's wife and share my life with a partner is strong. Just the other day, I reconnected with an old friend and this very topic came up. We were talking about my travel plans throughout Africa. She has been to several countries, so I was telling her about my shortlist of potential places to call home in the coming years. Do you know what she told me? She said that she can't just pick up and go anywhere anymore because she has her husband to consider. I don't envy her because I don't have those headaches to deal with. If I decided I was done with American politics tomorrow, I can sell my stuff and call a new country "home" relatively easily.

It's true what they say that single people wish to be married and married people wish to be single. Of course, this isn't the case for everyone. I think it's all about doing things in proper timing. As much as I try to convince myself that I'm ready for marriage, I know it's a lie. Are you courageous enough to admit that to yourself?

I understand that I'll have to consider my husband more important than myself. I recognize that it will no longer just be about me, but it will be about my family. There are still parts of me that love being able to do what I want when I want. I can leave the dishes in the sink for a night or two, order in because I don't feel like cooking, and let the laundry pile up until I only have one pair of clean jeans. It's great! Of course, there are other aspects of marriage beyond household chores; I just appreciate being able to have my home exactly how I like it.

Friend, if you remember nothing else from this chapter, remember that marriage is for God. The union you enter into with your husband is to give God glory. Your gifts and talents were designed to complement each other. Don't get so caught up in the other stuff.

Even if you're 50 and have never been kissed by a man, it's ok. Live a life that will glorify our Father. If He should allow you to have an earthly companion in the form of a spouse, then your priority is to serve God together. Can you promise that you'll remember this the next time the world attempts to tell you that something's wrong with you because you've reached a certain age and are still unmarried? We aren't meant to look or live like everyone else. You stand strong, and don't be afraid to stand out. After all, you're not standing alone.

FRIDAY NIGHT FEARS

Your life is a gift meant to be embraced and lived. You're allowed to not follow the path of those around you. What you do on your weekends may look vastly different than what everyone else does. Friend, do your utter best to find balance.

While I desire for you to succeed in this world, do not do so at the expense of anything. A career is valuable, but it shouldn't cause you to be alone. If you find yourself so consumed with your job and climbing that proverbial corporate ladder, then I want you to take some time to assess what true happiness in life looks like. Paying your bills is important, but it's also good to have a social life.

For quite some time I felt like an outsider because my peers were out having fun on the weekends, but I was working or writing academic papers. I yearned for a boyfriend just so I'd have something to do with someone on a Friday night. You may think it's weird that you're almost always home. You may believe that you're the only one staying in while the rest of the world is out "turning up." You're not. It's not. Friday night fears are a figment of our imaginations. If your only reason for entering into a relationship is to avoid being alone, then I suggest you take some time to discover why that is the case.

You've just finished a long work week. Your boss may have been harder on you this time because there is a major project due. You've been running non-stop because you're planning a huge event and it has been one crisis after another that you've had to resolve. When Friday night comes, please rest. Do not concern yourself with going out because you think it's what you should do. Instead, grab a good book, turn on a movie, order in, or enjoy your own company.

I can't stress enough the importance of getting to know yourself and liking the woman that you are before a mate comes into the picture. Why? Because no man can complete you. He will not always know what to do or say to make you feel better. Going out on a Friday night just to be seen really doesn't mean much. Most importantly, you shouldn't feel like a loser or a failure for not having plans. Now, don't misunderstand me. I'm not saying that you should be in the house every Friday night and never "put yourself out there" to meet new people. It's about balance.

Can I tell you a secret? I covet my Friday nights so much that sometimes I go out of my way **not** to make plans with anyone. It all started towards the end of my senior year at Howard. I led an active life back then with networking events at embassies, business meetings, regular church functions, and so on. My schedule was always so packed that the only way I could have any rest was to turn off my cell phone and remove myself from the madness. Life was just incredibly hectic in those days.

After event planning and attending died down, I'd begin to feel sad because no guy was asking me out or interested in doing anything on Friday nights. My friends almost always had plans. I was so busy with my own stuff that they found ways to occupy themselves without me. (I guess that happens when you have that person in your life who consistently turns down your invitations to hang out.) I wondered what was wrong with me because I was usually home on Friday nights when those seasons of heavy networking and events had come to an end. Without receiving an answer to my question, I began to maximize the time alone by having "me weekends." At first, I did them to mitigate Friday night fears, but I continued with these private sessions when I needed to get away from my busy schedule.

During those times, I got to know myself. Does that sound weird? How did I do it? One week I'd treat myself to a nice dinner at a restaurant I'd never visited. The next weekend, I ate at a different restaurant. As this continued, I learned quickly that I preferred certain cultural dishes and opened my palate to a world of flavors (literally). Thai calamari scores a little higher on my preference scale than Italian. Gulab jamun from India is one of my favorite desserts, not necessarily Turkish baklava. Although the thought of a foot massage is seemingly appealing, I'd much rather have a Swedish massage. The best *Sisterhood of the Traveling Pants* movie was the first one because the storyline and acting was so much stronger. Also, I'll watch just about any movie with Sanaa Lathan or Sandra Bullock because their acting skills are on point.

Did you learn something new about me just now? I hope so. I also pray that you will allow yourself to discover new things about yourself. Spending Friday nights by yourself is not a curse or punishment. You, dear friend, are a complex creature. There are so many things about you that even your closest friends may not know. Do not fool yourself into believing that the world goes out and parties on the weekends without you. It's your time to get to know, understand, and love the stunning, intelligent, fierce, and powerful woman that you are.

self is not a curse or punishment. You, dear friend, are a complex creature. There are so many things about you that even your closest friends may not know. Do not fool yourself into believing that the world goes out and parties on the weekends without you. It's your time to get to know, understand, and love the stunning, intelligent, fierce, and powerful woman that you are.

almost always had plans. I was so busy with my own stuff that they found ways to occupy themselves without me. (I guess that happens when you have that person in your life who consistently turns down your invitations to hang out.) I wondered what was wrong with me because I was usually home on Friday nights when those seasons of heavy networking and events had come to an end. Without receiving an answer to my question, I began to maximize the time alone by having "me weekends." At first, I did them to mitigate Friday night fears, but I continued with these private sessions when I needed to get away from my busy schedule.

During those times, I got to know myself. Does that sound weird? How did I do it? One week I'd treat myself to a nice dinner at a restaurant I'd never visited. The next weekend, I ate at a different restaurant. As this continued, I learned quickly that I preferred certain cultural dishes and opened my palate to a world of flavors (literally). Thai calamari scores a little higher on my preference scale than Italian. Gulab jamun from India is one of my favorite desserts, not necessarily Turkish baklava. Although the thought of a foot massage is seemingly appealing, I'd much rather have a Swedish massage. The best *Sisterhood of the Traveling Pants* movie was the first one because the storyline and acting was so much stronger. Also, I'll watch just about any movie with Sanaa Lathan or Sandra Bullock because their acting skills are on point.

Did you learn something new about me just now? I hope so. I also pray that you will allow yourself to discover new things about yourself. Spending Friday nights by your-

Here are some things that I did on Friday nights during my "me weekends." Would you be open to trying any of them? What else would you add to this list?

- Visit different ethnic restaurants
- Try a new activity (i.e. indoor rock climbing, paintballing, laser tag, snow tubing)
- Go to a spa for a massage or facial
- Watch movies by a certain producer, with a central theme, or containing a specific actor/actress
- Go to a spoken word or live music event
- Use a music streaming service to have your own concert and explore tunes from another region or genre
- Tour a museum
- Attend a festival
- Buy something from IKEA and put it together
- Hone your cooking skills by trying a new recipe

_____

_____

_____

_____

_____

_____

BEING THE UNWELCOMED STRANGER

One of the best things about being single in my early 20s was having the ability to pick up my stuff and move to different places. Sometimes it was a town 20 minutes down the road, and other times it was a city halfway around the country.

Before graduating from college, I'd stumbled upon a blog by a young Mexican American woman who trekked around the world doing odd jobs and freelancing. To say that I admired what this woman did would be an understatement. While I didn't necessarily want to emulate her in every regard, I did see value in exploring new cities in my 20s. Why not? I was single, had no children, and could easily use my skills to find a job virtually anywhere. Looking back, I think reading about her adventures opened a world of possibilities to me about other paths in life.

One of the worst things about being single in my early 20s was having the ability to pick up my stuff and move to different places. That seems like a contradiction of what I just said, right? It is. If I'm honest, it is frightening moving to a place where you know absolutely no one. However, it doesn't have to stay that way for long. Eventually, you will learn the lay of the land and make friends. Nevertheless, there are times when you will feel like you don't belong or are unwanted.

Not everyone will like you. There, I said it. Did you receive it? I need you to because it will help you in moments when you just don't understand people. There are simply some individuals in this world who will always find something to not like about you. They'll say you have a weird laugh, criticize your outfit choices, or indiscreetly comment on how "uptight" you are. That's ok. What you shouldn't do is listen to them and adjust accordingly.

You, my dear, were made in the image of God. There is nothing about you that is lacking or unworthy. Understanding your value is something that can never be overstated. Why? Because when you know and love yourself, you can handle moving to a community where you don't know anyone. When that happens, you become the stranger. It's an opportunity to be who you want and even transform into someone else. While I pray that you will stay true to who you are and allow those folks to love you for you, I pray even more that you will find those specific people who will welcome you with open arms.

From one who has been a stranger several times, I say to you (again) that not everyone will like or understand you. Better yet, not every person you meet will be happy you're there. People are people. That's probably never going to change. We stay guarded to protect ourselves from hurt.

When I moved to Georgia, I didn't always tell people that it was a decision that came out of intense prayer with God. A year prior to the move, I knew a major change was on its way because I had that sense I usually get before I relocate to a new place. However, I had no idea where God was leading. My life in Jersey was comfortable: I had solid clients, my friends and family were within a 30-minute drive from my condo, and I'd just begun attending a church where the pastor's Bible teachings were legit. Why would God want me to move? I didn't understand.

During one of the Friday night prayer sessions I faithfully attended with some incredible prayer warriors, I literally started bawling out of nowhere because I felt that the change was going to be in the form of a move; God was asking me to leave my friends and family. After hearing "Atlanta" during a separate intense prayer session, I spent an entire year asking God to speak to my heart and confirm that I had heard Him correctly; I wanted to know what the big deal was about Georgia. Truthfully, a couple of times I pulled a Gideon and fleeced God (Judges 6) because I wanted to know beyond a shadow of a doubt that it was in fact Him telling me to completely uproot my life.

When I got to Georgia, I stuck out like a sore thumb. Because Atlanta has so many transplants (non-native people who move to a major city from other places), I probably would have had an easier time adjusting if I had settled there. However, I opted to live about 20 minutes outside of the city in a town that was geared towards families (by my assessment). My neighbors were native to Georgia and many had never traveled outside of the state.

It was awkward telling people that I moved to Georgia because God told me to. Some people got it immediately, but the majority gave me blank stares like I'd grown two heads right in front of their eyes. I mean, their follow-up response made me feel like they had already labeled me as a weirdo. Thinking back to those moments, I realize I don't spend much time with the ones who didn't get it.

Things don't make sense to people sometimes. We need to be ok with that. Imagine: to a person who has never ventured outside of his or her hometown, me saying I moved 13 hours away (by car) from the ones I love sounds totally weird. It just doesn't make sense. Then, once I say that God had been telling me to do it for a whole year, they become even more confused. They just don't know what to do with this information. Hence, I am seemingly unwelcomed because some people I meet don't understand why anyone would live life the way I choose to.

Never assume you know someone's story without speaking to that individual yourself. A person may have once enjoyed welcoming strangers but became bitter when eventually his or her new friends moved on to a new town. If it happens enough times, that same person may just give up trying to meet new people out of fear of getting too close and experiencing the loss of yet another good friend. If that's the case, they are totally justified in not wanting to embrace you.

I think my expectations for how I should have been received when I relocated to new cities were simply too high. I guess it's because the decision to pick up and go was so huge for me that I was confident God had an entire community excitedly waiting for me to join them. That won't always be the case. Finding your "tribe" takes time. You may have moments when you're discouraged because you don't feel like you "fit" in anyone's world. Sometimes, your entrance will be quiet until you discover your place. Then, there will be much fanfare upon your exit.

You will have moments when you question if God really called you to that area, even though you know full well that He did. I think it's because we equate these big changes with the quality of our social interactions; that needs to change. If God says to go teach in Madagascar, you should go. If the people don't welcome you when you get there, then finish what you set out to do and leave. The area where I often lose my step is when it comes to keeping my purpose as the focus. Once I begin to dwell on how the community isn't responding to me the way I want, the quality and selflessness behind my service comes into question (my pride kicks in).

I wouldn't exactly call myself a social butterfly, but I get along well with people. I've been told there's something about my nature that attracts others. Although I enjoy being around people (most of them), I don't get my energy from socializing. My best times are when I'm in my apartment enjoying my own company. With that said, I get lost when the project is going so well that I want to share the news with someone. If no one is around, I go into a rut about the unfriendliness of the community, despite the fact that I've made little effort to integrate myself into the lives of others. This is normal. Do yourself a favor and observe the interactions of those in the community to identify one or two who you could get along with. Then, be bold and vulnerable enough to get to know them and allow them to get to know you. From there, if you all click, a friendship will naturally blossom.

The struggle comes when you have made strides to be included, but no one seems to involve you in much of anything. I once lived in a city where the people from a church I had been attending quickly learned that I had no family or friends in the area. Through a series of conversations, I learned that the group of women in what I hoped would become my new church community often socialized and went out together. I was never invited to attend any of these outings. It hurt. The worst part was that it was made known that I wasn't included, yet no steps were taken to rectify the alleged oversight. It continued for a series of weeks, which turned into months. Eventually, I stopped attending that church because I had specifically prayed for God to lead me to a community that would embrace me; this church wasn't what I had prayed for.

As the end of the year approached, I found it to be the hardest because I was alone. Here I was literally without any loved ones around to even spend the holidays with because a ticket to Jersey was way more than I was able to afford. (I forgot that I had to fly home for Christmas and waited too long to book a reasonably priced ticket.) Not one person I had met personally or professionally even considered extending any sort of offer to me to be their honorary family member for the day. That's the way it will be sometimes.

If I'm honest, not feeling like I belong somewhere is something that wrecks me. I don't think it's enough to say that this is a "millennial thing" because we all have a deep desire to feel like we are part of a group. The feeling of loneliness or being unwanted, when dwelled upon and allowed to fester, can be sometimes fatal. In circumstances where no one reaches out, I definitely feel unwelcomed. Maybe it's me, but I think just extending an invitation to a new person in town over the holidays or for a simple meal majorly boosts that individual's sense of belonging and community.

If you ever find yourself being the unwelcomed stranger, don't sweat. Use the time to get to know yourself better. You can explore new restaurants, take hikes and walks in nature, read more books, talk to God, or spend time in silence to center yourself. Jesus wasn't welcomed by all, nor were the disciples. I think what helps me the most is being intentional about doing activities I sincerely enjoy; sometimes I meet cool people who have mutual interests.

It's taken a lot of time to get to this place where I'm alright being by unwelcomed in a new city. Please don't think that something's wrong with you because you feel a sense of lack when no one reaches out. Just know that you aren't alone and that many of us have similar thoughts and feelings. Choosing to be proactive and allow yourself to be in positions where you can experience joy is what makes the difference.

FRIENDLESS

One of the thoughts that overtakes me at this age revolves around friendship. I guess it's something I took for granted as a child—growing up in a public school system where I literally saw my friends at least five days a week. We had many of the same classes, sat together at lunch, and passed each other in the hallways.

Making friends as a young adult can be challenging. In college I found myself trying to discover where I fit in. I rejected belonging to one clique, so I often flowed in various friend circles. If you ask me, it's a little boring to only be categorized as one "type." In any case, those friendships meant a lot to me because we experienced some of life's greatest pleasures and losses together. We supported each other, spent late nights studying for exams, and cooked some amazing food together.

Suffice it to say, when I relocated to a new place, I didn't have these types of relationships. I was friendless. As a full-fledged adult, I genuinely struggled to make friends. At times I thought I was too self-aware or self-confident, so people found that unattractive. Other times I wondered whether the culmination of my life experiences had made me into someone incapable of fitting in anywhere.

Although I detest labeling myself, there's a term for people like me. I use it occasionally when trying to explain the world from my perspective: third culture kid (TCK). As a TCK, I was born in one country but raised in another for most of my life. At home, I spoke Krio, ate Sierra Leonean food, and was raised as if I was still in Africa. At school, I got into discussions about pop culture, had American history drilled into my head, and listened to Trin-i-Tee 5:7, Lifehouse, Hoobastank, and Switchfoot. I no longer lived in Sierra Leone, so I didn't have a 100 percent, bona fide "African childhood." Still, I couldn't identify as 100 percent American either because so much of how I was brought up differed in comparison to my friends with an American passport.

Somewhere along the way, in figuring out my identity (before I even knew the label TCK existed), I created a third culture that was an amalgamation of the two worlds. I could easily flow between them, depending on who I was with and what was going on. Being a TCK, I developed a strong love for all things having to do with culture. It was easy to make friends with people from different countries because we could always find a shared experience. However, I quickly learned that I didn't typically function well in non-diverse communities.

When I moved to the West Coast, I was more than comfortable hanging out with the immigrant families; however, I had a tough time relating to the Americans. Now that I'm in the South, it takes a lot out me to find a common denominator when interacting with black Americans. It's not to say that we have nothing to discuss or no foundation to rely on for a friendship—it's more that I can't always relate or contribute to certain conversations. That is all to say that when I moved to these new cities, I found myself friendless more often than not.

Repeat after me: "I am never alone." Did you repeat it? Let's try it again. **I am never alone.** I can't tell you how many times in the course of the past decade I've had to remind myself (or have others remind me) of that simple truth. Moving from place to place in my 20s was exciting, but it came at a cost.

Friend, I highly recommend that you pick up and move to a place where you know absolutely no one at least once during your single years. Live among the people, take in the sights, and immerse yourself in a culture that is completely unfamiliar. It's a beautiful thing.

I pray you're afforded opportunities to do this internationally because it will alter your perspective on life. However, if you can't leave the continental US, then do it on the opposite coast. Why? Because the little corner of the world you live in is not all there is. In front of you is a world of fascinating people to be met, new experiences to be had, and amazing food to be consumed. Doesn't that sound exciting? It is!

Let's be clear, moving to a new city doesn't mean dropping the friends from your old city. It does mean, however, that they aren't as easily accessible to you. Yes, with the Internet and technology you could find ways to communicate, but it's not the same. The friendship temporarily suffers, and you all must adjust to not being as involved in each other's lives like before. It's only an issue if none of you try to make it work. Otherwise, the relationship should be fine.

Out of every topic we've covered so far, this is the one that's toughest to write. I pray that days of feeling friendless are few and far in between because I need you to understand in the innermost part of your being that the world and people in it do not define you. Your worth is not measured by the number of followers you have or how many people like your posts and pictures.

There are people who only desire to see you fail. These same individuals may pose as your friends, but they are not. One thing my mother instilled in me growing up was that I must choose my friends wisely. She always told me this before a new school year began, and it wasn't until I got older that I really understood why she drilled it into my head. It's often said that our friends are reflections of who we are, and I believe this to be true. Selecting good people who encourage us to be better versions of ourselves and motivate us to achieve the impossible is the difference between a successful future and a life of regret. Who knew our friends played such a vital role?

I know you yearn to be loved and feel like you belong, but don't let that be your reason for living. I pray, with all that is within me, that you have at least one person in your life who is a true friend. Someone who stands by you when others talk bad about you, your church family picks sides, or you're in a mood and act totally out of character. All you need is one real friend who knows your flaws and loves you anyway.

Feeling friendless is ok. It's something you and God can overcome together. But know that many of us go through it. I've lived in a few places. There have been several times when I just packed up my stuff and moved to a city where I knew no one. I was completely alone. My days were spent crying because I had no community. When this happens, consider spending more time with God and deepening that relationship. That's one way you'll make it as you grow older and remain unmarried.

I used to hold people in very high regard. If I made plans with someone, I got my hopes up, cleared my schedule, and counted down until the day we were supposed to hang out. This made it heartbreaking for me when the person cancelled at the last minute. I felt such disappointment when those calls, texts, or emails came. I became bitter and stopped believing people would follow through on their word. I wrote people off after they bailed on me once with excuses that I didn't deem acceptable. Do you know what my problem was? I was allowing my social life to rule me.

People will disappoint you; it is our nature. When sin entered the world through Adam and Eve, so did a whole host of other things. We're selfish, egotistical, quick to anger, jealous, and so much more. We put our needs before others, yet we expect them to go out of their way for us when we don't even think to do the same in return.

Friendlessness can also take on another form. What I'm talking about is the feeling of being alone when there are people around, but none of them are available. It's that feeling you get when you have news and want to share it, but you realize you have to pick up the phone or send a text because the people who would celebrate with you are hundreds, or thousands, of miles away. It's feeling like you can't just chill with those in your current friend circle because they see you as a professional acquaintance; they wouldn't dare to cross the firmly drawn relationship boundary lines.

On many occasions I've tried to befriend women I met in a professional context. My attempts to get us to learn about each other's interests and have conversations that weren't business-related failed miserably. That's just the way it goes sometimes, I guess. We never know a person's entire history until he or she shares it, so we can't expect them to be as open to new things or people as we are. Some are more comfortable knowing each other in only one context, while others see no problem with blurring the lines.

Friend, there may be many days when you may feel like the relationship boundaries are overwhelming and venture to utter the words "I have no friends." Don't. Don't you dare. You can think it and even write it down for a moment (be sure to tear that paper up later). Never, ever say it out loud. You are **not** friendless. You are **not** unloved. People care about you. God cares about you.

I don't know where you are in your faith walk, but I know that (whether you believe in Him for yourself or not) God is always there. He sees you when you shed those tears at night because you came home and had no one to congratulate you on that promotion. He hears you when you vent about that person who is only pretending to support you so that you'll connect them with some people in your rolodex. He knows how you feel when you look at your bank account to see money in there, yet you still feel unfulfilled.

Think back to the last time you felt friendless. What was going on? Were you nailing every task or assignment and feeling like the queen of the world? When everything was completed and you had a moment to breathe, is that when the thoughts came? That's usually what happens with me. But I am reminded that God says He will never leave me (Deuteronomy 31:6). I'm never really alone because the friend who sticks closer than a brother is always with me (Proverbs 18:24).

You're never friendless. The people you're used to having around may not be there when you want them to be, but there are those who will drop everything they're doing if you just made it known that you needed them. I have this tendency not to say what I need in relationships. I hope that you're not the same way. It's ok to be vulnerable and tell someone that you want to spend time with him or her. Sometimes that's how the best friendships are formed. I know the individuals I've allowed to get close to me have shared how much they have valued me letting them get past my walls.

With every relocation, I learn something about myself when it comes to relationships. I don't always fight to keep people in my life, but it leads to something beautiful when I do. Some friendships have survived the moves because we determined to stay in each other's lives. Other relationships eventually faded because the distance was too great. But I know if I returned to those places tomorrow, we would pick up from where we left off. Learn to be ok with the ebbs and flows of friendships in this season; the ones meant to last a lifetime will.

There is a season for everything. If a friendship feels like it's been drifting for some time and there's no saving it, let it go. There have been a few in my own life that have gone that way, but in some bizarre way we reconnect and continue building on our previous relationship to make it stronger than before. When that happens, I suspect that it is God's divine intervention at work.

Friendship is a tricky thing to navigate, but you can do it. Do not ever feel like you're friendless. (I can't stress this enough.) Do you know that you never are? God is always there for you. When you're sad and just desire to feel loved, He's around. I tend to forget this often. I hope you never will. Just call on Him and begin talking; He's always listening.

Here are some things that I do when I begin to feel friendless. Have you tried any of these? What would you add to this list?

- Listen to uplifting music
- Read the Bible
- Watch a sermon (usually by Priscilla Shirer)
- Read a book for leisure
- Call a trusted friend for an honest, vulnerable conversation

PUTTING ON THE WEIGHT AGAIN

As I approached age 30, I began noticing that my body responded to food differently. It took a few years for me to finally get it and decide to do something about it. To be completely honest, it took a conversation with a dear woman who is more like an older sister to me to realize that something had to change. I think the words she expressed were received well because somewhere in my heart of hearts I knew that my health was not a priority in my life.

There are few things we can actually control in this world. On that list is our ability to change how we manage our health. I learned in high school and college that stress takes a serious toll on my body (probably more than the average person). Namely, I tend to overeat when I have too many deadlines or projects in the pipeline. I noticed after undergrad that I had to pay close attention to how often I ordered takeout during the week. Not only did it hurt my wallet, it was also a huge factor in my putting on excessive weight. The thing about weight, as you may know, is that it's easy to put on. Taking it off is the real pain.

Friend, I never want you to feel like you aren't beautiful because you gained a few pounds; that's not what I'm saying. Even as I write this chapter, I am in a place where I am working to shed some of this weight to become a healthier me. This chapter about weight is to help you identify patterns in your life that can be detrimental to your health. You may be built with wide hips and curves for days. Alternatively, you may have a thinner frame. That doesn't matter. What's important is that you're healthy and happy. Know the signs to look for that help you recognize when life is spinning out of control so that your health isn't compromised.

It's important to have healthy eating habits and feel like you are making wise decisions. There's something about life that you feel good when you look good. We shouldn't just **feel** good, though. We need to **be** good. Know that you won't always be in control of things. You won't always get your way. But make it a goal to maintain certain lifestyle practices that will benefit you in the long run.

Let me be real—food is the first thing I turn to when life feels out of my control. Is it the same for you? Have you noticed that you cook less or make unwise eating decisions when your schedule seems chaotic? Is this an area of struggle? I'll be the first to tell you that this should not be the case. I know it seems like there are easier things to do, and most days you just want to eat someone else's food. But think about the long-term impact.

Do you know what I am doing to help get my weight under control? I put myself on a budget. Each week I give myself $20 for eating out. It's not a huge amount, but I can still treat myself after a long week. I can eat whatever I want for the whole weekend or just one day. The only stipulation is that I cannot spend more than $20. Of course, some weeks I go over a little (or a lot), but the key is to exercise as much discipline as possible to maintain consistency. I challenge myself to stay on this budget for several weeks at a time to see how long I can go.

Next, I force myself to work out by saying, "Just get in the car and drive." This is what I would tell myself In Jersey after getting off the train or driving home from my last client for the day. I kept a duffel bag with my clothes and gym sneakers in the trunk of my car practically every day. If I intended to go to the gym, I made sure I had a bottle of water with me. Once I finished working for the day, I'd get in the car to go home and say, "Just get in the car and drive." I'd repeat this phrase to myself until I reached the exit for the gym. Then, just as if I was on autopilot, I'd take the turn and end up in the parking lot of my local gym. I was already there and had my stuff in the car, so I might as well go inside to get a workout in. Right? Right!

The mind is so complex yet so simple. After a few weeks of getting in the car and driving to the gym, I found myself adding extra workout days to my routine. I was actually looking for ways to make trips to the gym to work out. I woke up earlier and went to bed later just to make sure I exercised that day. It worked! Once I settled into my routine of healthier eating and exercising, I began to feel a million times better.

When it comes to healthy living, another thing I do is replace one meal with a salad (usually for dinner). This worked great when I lived in South Jersey. I'd go to the gym after a long day at work, exercise for 30-45 minutes, then get out a medium-sized bowl to make a Caesar salad. It was a pretty simple recipe: romaine lettuce, Caesar dressing, croutons, and sometimes parmesan cheese. The trick is to measure your croutons and salad dressing so that you have more leaf than fat and carbs. It worked like a charm, and I saw the weight melt off fairly quickly.

Friend, do not neglect your health. God has given us one body, and it is our job to take care of it. If I had my way, I would have never allowed processed sugars to ever touch my lips from childhood. They are the most dangerous of all sugars. Also, I would have been more careful with my soda consumption when I was younger.

You may need to hire a professional to help educate you about your body type and health. There's no shame in that because, ultimately, you're taking steps to better yourself. Make sure you're actually learning from what they're teaching, though. If not, look for someone else who will take the time to explain things to you.

Finding out the root cause of your poor eating habits makes a world of difference. I know that I make unwise decisions when I take on too much and neglect properly fueling my body. My metabolism doesn't work like everyone else's. I can't stress enough how important it is to know and spend time with yourself to discover these things. Here's to a happier, healthier you!

CROOKED CROWN

Confession: I don't particularly like it when women refer to themselves and others as "queens." I understand the rationale behind it and stand in support (kind of) because it makes sense, but I am a proponent of the meaning rather than the actual term. Is it just me? Probably.

Regardless of how I feel about the term, I'm going to go ahead and use it here because it's the best way to describe you. This chapter is devoted to you. I just wanted to remind you of some things. Ready? Here goes, **queen**.

You are **brilliant**. You may not have the mathematical mind of Katharine Johnson or a knack for computers like Evelyn Boyd Granville, but your brain is a complex organ best suited for you. No one else in the world thinks exactly like you. You're able to see things that others don't even understand.

You are **creative**. The way you use words to express your thoughts is mind blowing. The works of your hands to create beauty out of what others view as nothingness is incredible. You have an eye for color and design that turns the simplest of things into something extraordinary.

You are **loved**. It goes beyond the love that you receive from a parent. You are loved by the Creator; the One who cared so much for you that He sent Jesus to die on the cross of Calvary. You are so loved that there are people who petition heaven regularly on your behalf for God to grant you wisdom, protection, and favor.

You are **captivating**. It's more than just your physical beauty that draws people to you. They are attracted to your sense of wonder. The joy that emanates from your soul and your laughter that fills the room makes them long for your company.

There will be days when you feel like you've lost your way and times when you forget who you are. When you have those moments, I want you to stand in front of a mirror and remind yourself of who God has made you to be. You must encourage yourself because others may not. They will attempt to be there for you, but some may secretly be holding out or praying for your downfall.

It's also in this place of feeling like you have low self-worth that you may be prone to make unwise decisions. Do you know what your Achilles heel is? It is that thing or person that causes you to sin or make poor choices. The one who weakens your sense of right and wrong to enter the gray area. When our lives are in turmoil, things begin to feel out of control. Once we forget who we are, chaos ensues. Our crowns become crooked, and the decisions we make are highly questionable.

Want to know something? My area of weakness has always been romantic relationships with the opposite sex. I was raised in a home where I received love and attention from my father, so I don't think it was because I had "daddy issues." I suspect it became my weakness because that was the area that was most undeveloped in my early years. I didn't really pay guys much attention when I was in elementary and middle school. Yes, I had crushes and thought some boys in my classes were cute. But it never went beyond me simply admiring my friend of the opposite sex; beginning a real dating relationship was the last thing on my mind.

As I grew older, I had other priorities and didn't learn how to treat men I had feelings for. It wasn't until my mid-20's that I realized that I never respected the men I was romantically involved with. Not only that, I also struggled with relinquishing control to allow my romantic partner to play a serious role in my life. Basically, I got into relationships where everything was on my terms and didn't allow the man to have more significance than I deemed appropriate. How do you think that went? In all cases, the relationships ended. I was left with a broken heart that took months to heal. It became a pattern that I didn't recognize until I had the one relationship that nearly broke me. It was only then that I seriously spent time being introspective and seeking God for some answers.

My inability to let men in stemmed from my belief that I had to prove my worth by what I brought to the table to keep a man. I thought that if he saw how much of an asset I was to him and that I could fend for myself, then he would want me more. I didn't stroke his ego, praise him, or tell him any of my inner thoughts. While I was trying to show that I was worthy through my actions that delivered practical results, he was longing for my affection through words. It was a losing battle. To be fair, there were some other acceptable practices in modern dating relationships that some of the men wanted to engage in that I was not willing to perform. That was also a big contributing factor to why a few relationships ended.

There are several Bible stories I turn to when I feel like I need to be reminded about what love isn't. Love doesn't manipulate. I think about Samson and Delilah. Samson was so enamored by Delilah that he forgot who he was when he was with her. He wanted her to have a more vital role in his life, so he gave in and told her the secret behind his strength. She wasn't entirely innocent, though. She used her feminine ways to get him to cave and give her what she wanted. This one action of giving into Delilah's request ultimately led to his ruin.

David, King of Israel, lusted for Bathsheba to monumental proportions. After seeing her naked and enjoying it, he longed so badly for her that he became an adulterer. To make matters worse, he turned into a murderer when he plotted to kill Bathsheba's husband to cover up the pregnancy that resulted from his one-night stand with her. Can you believe it? This man slept with another man's wife, knocked her up, then placed her husband in a strategic battle position that was guaranteed to get him killed.

Are you seeing a pattern here that relationships with the opposite sex bring about the worst in us? That wasn't quite what I was getting at. Let's explore a different kind of story to see what love is.

Love is sacrificial. Jacob spent 12 years of his life working for Laban to earn Rachel's hand in marriage. Can you imagine? He was so convinced that Rachel was the woman for him that he sacrificed to have the opportunity to be with her. Even though I have issues with the notion of a man performing physical labor to get my father's permission to marry me, I think there's something beautiful about the gesture. Regardless of who it is, I think that there should be an element of sacrifice in my relationship with my spouse. If neither of us are making sacrifices to be with the other, I'd question our level of devotion to the marriage.

My longing to receive love from a life partner comes in ebbs and flows. I find that after I've put on an event, taught a Bible study, or done some sort of act of community service that I often go into a funk. Mine is caused because I truly desire a companion to share these things with. From there, my mind begins to wander and my self-esteem plummets. Forget the fact that I own a business, make enough to live on my own, and have a social circle of tried and true friends. None of that seems to matter in those moments because I'm not with someone. I allow my crown to become crooked when I forget who I am.

Friend, you are not lacking because you're unmarried. There's nothing wrong with you because suitors aren't knocking at your door. I challenge you to shift your thinking to discover why this area is one of such contention. Was it something about how you were raised? Maybe it had to do with what you saw in the movies? Only you can answer these questions. But I pray you'll discover the truth and fix your crown, queen.

STAND TALL, ANOMALY

Most of my life I've known that I was not like everyone else. I pray you never feel inadequate because you have so much to offer this world. I pray you never aim to fit society's mold because you were created to break it. There's nothing about you that was designed to be just like everyone else, so don't chase that desire. If everyone else is going after one thing, then you dare to be different by pursuing another.

In many ways, the knowledge that I was different from others has kept me out of a lot of trouble. Instead of going to parties in high school, I volunteered in the community. Rather than getting into relationships with guys, I led Bible studies. I can only attribute these things to God for preserving me from pain and heartache. I can imagine that if I had acted on impulses surrounding guys at a young age, that my life would have turned out differently.

In middle and high school, the media tells you that you're supposed to be hooking up, trying out drugs, partying, and all that. Movies and television go so far as to make it seem like that's the norm. The truth is that it's not. Most high schoolers aren't "sexing it up" or getting "totally wasted." This is not to say that there aren't schools in some towns where a large population of people do this; it's just not everywhere.

Do you have goals you want to accomplish? Does partying not fit into that plan? Fine! Are you working toward making a name for yourself in a specific field? Would having a boyfriend be a huge distraction? There's no mandate that you must live your life according to any person's manual. The only guide we've been given for this life is the Bible. Don't place yourself in a position where the distractions cause you to miss out on some wonderful adventures; pursue what is true for you.

What many people may not tell you is that a relationship requires work, time, and sacrifice. If you're not able to put someone else first in your life, then it's a little selfish to enter a relationship. I always come back to this when debating whether to date someone. If I can honestly answer that I am unwilling to carve out time in my schedule to be with a man, then it's unfair for me to make him think the relationship could become something long-lasting.

There is absolutely nothing wrong with choosing not to engage in behaviors and activities that you know will prevent you from making your dreams come true. Some professional athletes train so intensely that their careers come before anything else. Future politicians are often so busy with work and travel that they hardly have time for a relationship. Medical professionals work such insane hours that not many of them have opportunities to date outside of work. No one humiliates or shames people in these professions for having certain priorities. You shouldn't feel ashamed because you're pushing 30 (or well beyond) and are still single.

Stand tall, anomaly, because you are destined for greatness. Think back to something you really wanted some time ago. What was it? Why didn't you pursue it? What's preventing you from doing it now?

Work can't be an excuse. If you were willing to put in the work back then, I know you can do it now. Was it about the money? I understand this can be a huge barrier, but maybe there are some things you can cut back on to begin saving funds?

If it's not a project that requires more than a year to do, you may consider waking up a little earlier and going to bed a tad later on some days to carve more time into your day. As one who loves sleep, I know the sacrifice is all too real. Nevertheless, the victory of accomplishing your goals is even sweeter. How do I know? Because this book is one of my victories. The fact that you're reading it now brings tears to my eyes. These are words I longed to hear, and I'm grateful for women who spoke them to me at different times on my journey.

As you continue to grow, there will be many voices of influence around you. It's a little selfish, but I want to be the second loudest one (after God, of course). Through this book, I desire to be the voice reminding you that there is no one in this world like you. The one who tells you just how beautiful you are when the suitors don't come on Friday and Saturday nights to take you on a date. I want to cheer you on when you go for that promotion or land that deal that seemed impossible to get. I long to be your confidante when you're in a new city and feeling friendless.

Don't get me wrong. I don't want to be God. I really just yearn to be your number one cheerleader when you feel like there's no one in your corner. I wrote this book for you because I suspect you may have moments when you feel the way I have for so many years. Here's to you, brave soul, let the journey continue.

NO MORE CHASING

The chase. If you're like me, you probably don't even realize you're doing it until it's already begun. What does the chase look like? Well, it can take on many forms. For me, it sometimes involves downplaying my dreams and aspirations because I want to seem less ambitious. I've also gone days and weeks pretending I enjoyed certain sports, hobbies, and topics simply to appear like my interests aligned with those of a man I liked. Of course, it wasn't always a façade (I may have genuinely been open to an idea or activity), but sometimes the level of interest was exaggerated. In a few instances, the chase involved me acting like I didn't know how to do something just to allow a man to come and teach me or show off his physical prowess.

What is "the chase"? It's anything that we, as women, do to diminish who we are to try to get a man or capture his attention. I have literally downplayed my intelligence and allowed a man to waste countless hours of my life trying to figure something out instead of speaking up when I knew the obvious solution. Isn't that crazy?! I hope you're not like me.

Some older women have told me that I have to make a man feel like he's in control and leading the relationship.

I've long since stopped listening to that particular piece of advice. Why? Because I find that a man "leading a relationship" by God's standards has nothing to do with me pretending I don't have a brain. I, too, can contribute to the decisions that will impact the both of us.

The chase involves doing things out of your character to seem more desirable to men. Let's call it what it really is: faking. If I have to pretend to be someone I'm not to get a guy, then he's not worth it. I've been told by some people in my life that certain men from my past were intimidated by me. What does that even mean? I'm not going around lessening their manhood or anything. But I do encourage, support, and hold a man accountable for the things he says and does. Could that be the problem? Is that a real problem? I don't think so.

I'm coming to the table with a lot to offer and have made the most of my single years (or am attempting to), so I think it's more than acceptable that I desire someone who will value that. If that makes me seem intimidating, then so be it. The men who have a problem with that are definitely not for me. They meet me and hear about my accolades; then, they automatically think I want them to be like me. If I wanted to date myself, I wouldn't even bother with relationships.

Truthfully, I'm just so sick of men saying women who are capable of taking care of themselves are "intimidating." Aren't you tired of that rubbish label? The man who has the audacity to tell you that, is not worth it, dear friend.

He's basically letting you see his insecurity from the beginning; that seldom ever changes. He will always see you as out of his league and never feel that he measures up. You will drive yourself crazy trying to love him and show him that you're unconcerned about titles, income, and accolades, but it just won't click with him.

Although I haven't literally gone around following guys and doing too much to let them know I was interested, I am guilty of not allowing myself to see the signs and putting my heart on the line for men who couldn't handle my personality. This is a crucial part of the chase that isn't always talked about. A man could be making it very apparent that he doesn't want a romantic relationship, but we convince ourselves that he's just shy or afraid of rejection. We push and push until he reluctantly acquiesces to being with us, only for the relationship to turn sour shortly after. Can we stop doing that?

A former colleague once told me that I must be willing to let the guy I was crushing on pursue me. She said that this particular man was one who took his time making decisions. However, if I allowed him time to process and determine that I was the one he wanted, he would run after me with everything in him, until he caught me. Doesn't that sound romantic? It does to me.

That's what I want—a man who would stop at nothing to get my attention. He would be so convinced that he needed me in his life that he'd risk making a fool of himself. Don't misunderstand. I'm not talking about crazy stalkers.

I'm referring to a man who has prayed and knows that our union would be blessed by God.

The young man my former colleague and I talked about never ended up pursuing me. To be honest, I didn't exercise patience in allowing him to process and realize just how amazing our relationship could be (he was taking too long). But that situation taught me that I like decisive men and wouldn't have been able to handle him making decisions in a marriage. (I hear he has since found himself a woman who he has decided to pursue and wish him the best because I learned some valuable lessons about myself because of our friendship.)

That's the thing about the chase—once you're past the emotional intensity it brings, you get to do some serious self-reflection. During those times, you discover things about yourself you may have never known.

What does the chase look like for you? Have you noticed any patterns relating to how you deal with crushes on men? Do you find that you fake it to get a man? It's ok to be totally honest with yourself. There's no judgment because we're all guilty of engaging in this type of behavior.

I've decided that I won't chase anymore. I refuse to diminish my intelligence, accomplishments, and ambition because of fear that a man won't want me because I "do too much." I am made in the image of God. I am a daughter of the King of Kings. He has not created me to just exist and sit around waiting for a man to take notice of me. If a man can't handle me, then he's not the one God has for me. It's as simple as that.

Will you join me in declaring your refusal to engage in the chase? Will you determine that you will reject the world's notion that being 30 (or beyond) and single makes you less desirable? Will you agree to go after your dreams so hard that you will stop at nothing to make them come true? Will you allow God the opportunity to use your life to change the course of history from your small corner of the world? Let's continue defying 30 together!

WORDS FROM THE AUTHOR

Thank you so much for taking the time to read this book. I felt the need to write it because so much of our culture, especially church culture, still teaches that marriage is the ultimate goal in life. I desire this book to serve as a conversation starter in churches, ministry groups, and even on college campuses about singleness in today's world. If we are to change how society views single women over 30, then we must be intentional about speaking up about our experiences. Yes, our relationship status is important. But it shouldn't define who we are as women.

Also, I wanted to take a moment to explain the book cover briefly. The letters "SLN" on the woman's shirt stand for "single life navigator." In preparation for this book's release, I wanted to create a platform where we could share our life experiences as a way to cheer each other on. If you have a story to tell about how you're navigating your single years God's way, check out the blog at www.singlelifenavigator.com. I hope to hear from you soon!

www.ingramcontent.com/pod-product-compliance
Lightning Source LLC
Chambersburg PA
CBHW021121080526
44587CB00010B/591